DON'T JUDGE

DON'T JUDGE

Agnes Bonas

BOOKS ACADEMY
LEARNING LIFE FROM EVERY PAGE

Books Academy LLC
112 SW H K Dodgen Loop
Temple, Texas 76504
Hotline: (254) 800-1189

Ordering Information:
Quantity sales. Special discounts are available on quantity purchases by corporations, associations, and others. For details, contact the publisher at the address above.

Printed in the United States of America.

ISBN-13:   Paperback   978-1-966567-09-7
              eBook   978-1-966567-10-3

Library of Congress Control Number:

Thank you, Father God, for giving me the strength, and stamina to rise above each situation that occurred in my life.

Everyone has a story, and everyone is going through something you don't even know. Don't be so quick to judge people by their outer appearance, because you don't know where you will find yourself in this world.

This is a true story. The names of the characters have been changed to protect the identities of the innocent in my story.

By Author
THE QUEEN OF INSPIRATIONAL QUOTES

Christine worked for an Insurance Company/Law Firm for 22 years. The Company was like a family. It was a home away from home and we all knew each other. We all attended weddings, birthday parties, pool parties, funerals, barbecues, baby showers; and they also knew who got divorced and who was caught cheating in motels and hotels, and who carried on secret lesbian affairs and homosexual love affairs while married. The Company Christine worked for all these years was sold to a giant corporation soon after some were let go with packages; others quit, others were forced out because of their age, and some were fired. Christine was one of them who got fired. Christine had her very own apartment at the time. She had just bought a new car and her life was good, so it seemed until her downfall. Christine's money ran out and she applied for Unemployment Benefits. Eventually her Unemployment Benefits ran out. Christine went through her 401K, and she was hit with stiff fines and penalties. Afterwards, she humbled herself and went to an Agency to ask for help. It took a lot out of her to go and ask for help. Christine was full of pride, but she had to humble herself to get the benefits that she needed to survive. Christine uploaded her resume online to get a job and you would think that after 22 years of experience, she would get a lot of call-backs or people wanting to hire her. Again, she was in for a rude awakening, and she was in for the hardest ride of her life.

Christine would often visit her mom on Sundays. They would often go out to eat at her favorite Diner for brunch. They enjoyed each other's company, and she would listen to her mom's conversation about her growing up and how she was mistreated as a child. It was very sad that her mom had been sexually molested, abused physically and mentally as a child. It was just

1

very sad. Christine would also notice little things about her mom like her mom forgetting the smallest of things. For example, her mom would get dressed on a Saturday thinking it was Sunday and going out to Church. Someone would eventually bring her back home. Christine failed to realize that Dementia was slowly showing its ugly face.

All of Christine's money ran out and so did all her friends who she had dinners and lunches with and those who used her as their very own personal chauffeur. Little did she know that she was going to move in with her mom and how much they would need each other. Moving in was very easy. Christine stayed with her for four years in her Senior Citizen Apartment. Being with her mom was not an easy task and they bumped heads often. Her mom was a Stylish, Stubborn, Strong, and a very Independent Woman. Christine stayed with her as her mom's memory was slowly decreasing, and of course, she was in denial. They would continually bump heads quite often. Her mom would misplace her things, and she would call the police on Christine and would say, "Christine stole my passport, my bank card, and my money!" The cops would show up, but when they saw the state Christine's mother was in, they knew it was Dementia. They would leave and say, "Mary your daughter is doing a good job taking care of you". That did not sit very well with her mom, and she went to the Housing Authority trying to have them put Christine out. Christine's mom would even run into the hallway and scream at the top of her lungs "Help! Murder! Police!" The cops would come and leave. Again, they knew they needed each other. At that point in time, Christine soon realized that God had her there for a purpose and that she was there and that was her assignment from God to take care of her mom. Christine knew she could not leave until she completed her assignment from God.

One day, Christine and her mom had a heated argument and what came out of her mom's mouth next shocked Christine to the core. She didn't know why she didn't collapse as her mom blurted out that Christine's dad while he was going back and forth working in Canada, he had an affair with a white woman and this woman had children with her dad. Wow, that was very hard to swallow for Christine, because now she had biracial half-brothers or half-sisters, whom she didn't even know. She didn't even know their ages, their likes or dislikes, or what they looked like. Christine told God if God wanted her to meet her half-siblings, God would make a way for her to meet them. Christine's dad died and he took that secret to his grave. Her mom made it known and she was not taking that secret to her grave.

As time went on, Christine's mom's memory was deteriorating slowly and her favorite time together was spent at the Diner, watching her favorite TV show, and eating her favorite junk food was also going slowly. As her mom's health started to decline, she was still very stubborn. There was a time she would just pass out wherever she was, and someone would bring her back home or sometimes Christine just had to pick her up like a baby and put her on the bed. Thank God, Christine's mom was a small person, and she weighed no more than 99 pounds. Christine would ask her what happened, and her mom would say that's "None of your business." "Why are you asking me my business?" Again, this woman was still tough and had a fast mouth. Christine was tougher and was not going to back down either. There were times Christine would come home and find her suitcase in the living room, and she knew what that meant. Get out!

The Agency at that time sent Christine to a Daycare to work just for four hours two days a week. Christine could not figure out why God wanted her to be there. When Christine got there, she soon realized what God wanted her to see. She observed that some of the kids needed help, some had speech impairment and learning disabilities and some were slower than the other kids, and they were all put together. Some got the help they needed, and some were lost along the way in the shuffle and some of the parents were in denial. One of the teachers was bipolar and she said because of a certain healthcare, she could not afford to take her medication, which was scary. When that certain teacher spoke with those kids, trust me, they would run and do as they were told to do. Then you had the teachers who would gossip about whose parents were separated, divorced, who were on drugs, who brought from home frozen breast milk at the daycare for a two-year-old boy to drink from his sippy cup. Then you have a teacher who would scream at a little girl. This teacher would say things like "I hate you!" The little girl was in tears and her mom had twins at home, so all the attention left her and went to the twins at home. Christine looked at the little girl who had big blue eyes and curly blond hair. Christine realized this teacher was jealous of this little girl for how she looked. How can an adult be jealous of a three-year-old? Most parents who leave their children at a Daycare to go to work are playing Russian Roulette with their children's lives. Christine was silent, because all she could do was to lay her hands on their heads and ask God to bless, guide, and protect them. She didn't say it loudly because some of these kids were learning to talk and they would repeat everything that was being said to them, and some were Jewish.

Christine left the Daycare center because her mom needed her more. Christine investigated her mom's Insurance, and the Insurance started paying Christine to take care of her mom. So now she was under the A Program which paid family members to take care of their loved ones. She was home again taking care of her mom. Christine left one Friday to go to Church and while she was in Church, her brother called her at Church and said the Ambulance and the Police were at the apartment and their mom was not feeling well. When Christine got home, she asked her what happened and her mom said, "Why did you leave me alone?" Christine guessed that her mom needed her attention. Going to Church now was out of the question for four years. Christine spent most of her days taking care of her mom. The A Program paid her for six hours, seven days a week, and the rest of the hours were on her. Everything was on Christine; she stayed with her mom 24 hours a day 7 days a week. Christine also noticed that when her mom would use the bathroom, she would pass a lot of blood. Christine and her brother finally took their mom to the doctor and the doctor took samples of blood from their mom to find out what was the problem. The doctor called Christine and told her that her mother's blood was very low, and that she had to be admitted immediately into the hospital. The next day Christine and her brother took their mom to the hospital where she was admitted for 5 days. The hospital ran many tests, and they wanted to operate, but Christine's brother said, "No", because their mom was 89 years old. The Hospital kept their mom in the Hospital for 5 days and they gave her nine pints of blood. While Christine's mom was in the hospital, the Nurses would say to her that her mom was very sneaky, because she would get out of bed and try to use the bathroom all by herself and the alarm on the bed would go off. The IV, she would try to pull it out so they had to put mittens on both of her hands so that she would leave the IV alone. They tried doing a Colonoscopy on her, but her heart rate dropped so they decided not to do the Colonoscopy. They also did a series of tests on her to find out what was the problem. The problem they found was that Christine's mom had Cancer in the Colon and this dreaded disease was now spreading to her liver. There's no history on Christine's mom side of the family with Cancer. This was going to be a long and rough ride for both Christine and her mom. The doctor spoke to both Christine and her brother at the hospital. The doctor said it could be a week or a couple of months because no one knew how long she had to live. They decided to take their mom home. Christine and her bother could not put their mom in a Nursing Home because she would die faster. So, they took her home. Christine called the Agency, and a Case Worker arrived, and a Nurse came to evaluate Christine's mom, and after their visit, they sent over to the Apartment oxygen air tanks, a wheelchair, a commode, a hospice bed and a box full of medication.

Christine said to God, HOW AM I GOING TO DO THIS?

> CHRISTINE WAS NOW THE NURSE FOR HER MOM.

> CHRISTINE WAS NOW THE COOK FOR HER MOM.

> CHRISTINE WAS NOW THE HOUSE CLEANER FOR HER MOM.

CHRISTINE WAS NOW THE SECRETARY WHO KEPT ALL THE DOCTOR APPOINTMENTS FOR HER MOM.

CHRISTINE WAS NOW THE BANKER FOR HER MOM.

CHRISTINE WAS NOW THE HAIR STYLIST FOR HER MOM.

CHRISTINE WAS NOW THE MAKEUP ARTIST FOR HER MOM.

CHRISTINE WAS NOW THE ERRAND AND THE DELIVERY PERSON FOR HER MOM.

Christine also did laundry for her mom. Laundry had to be done three days a week because of the heavy passing of urine. Christine had to force her mom to wear Depends which was a battle; but at the end, Christine won the battle. Christine took care of her mom twenty-four hours a day seven days a week which was very exhausting. She also took care of her finances. Christine's life was put on hold for four long years. But through the storm, she managed to write and publish her first book which is entitled, "The Queen of Inspirational Quotes" which she considers that book to be her baby. Christine would have her computer on her lap and her mom would be lying next to her on the hospice bed. Christine did receive positive feedback from both friends and family who purchased and read her book. Christine also completed several courses, and she is also a Licensed Motivational Speaker, Licensed Counselor, an Ordained Minister, and she received her degree in Theology. While struggling to take care of her mom without the help of her three brothers, sometimes Christine would get cursed out if she didn't move fast enough to attend to her mother's needs. By now, she was used to being treated like crap. But she knew it was her assignment and eventually, the assignment would come to an end.

As time went on, Christine's mom's health was deteriorating rapidly, because she had to clean her up, she now had to take a pair of scissors to cut the Depends on her mom off her, her legs were so wobbly. Christine had to pick her up like a baby to clean her. Her mom was no longer talking and no longer eating or drinking anything. Christine tried forcing her to drink something, but she would throw it up, because at that time, her mom could no longer talk. Christine would rub her head and kiss her hands. On December 14, 2016, Christine got up at 1:30 am in the morning and she went into the refrigerator to get her mom a drink, but she didn't take the drink. So, Christine decided that she was not going to waste the drink, so she drank it and went back to sleep. At 7:15 am in the morning, Christine said to her mom that she was going to make them some breakfast. Her mom didn't answer so she went over to her, and she touched her forehead, but it was cool. She put her index finger across her mom's nose, and she was not breathing; she placed her hands on her chest, and it was not moving up and down. Christine knew her mom had gone, and she believed she must have passed away between the hours of 3:00 am and 5:00 am. Christine took her hands and closed her mom's eyes, and she covered her with the Comforter on the bed. Christine called her brother and told him that their mom was dead, and her brother was in shock and screaming. Christine then called the Hospice Nurse, who she said the following to Christine, "If the bed is in an upright position, put the bed flat and if there's a pillow under her head, remove the pillow and flush the remaining medications down the toilet." While Christine was waiting for the Hospice Nurse to arrive, she got up and took a bath and went into the kitchen and made breakfast for herself. She was sitting on the couch with her mom's dead body beside her, while eating her breakfast. The Nurse arrived and signed the Death Certificate. The Death Certificate would be signed at the time of death when the Nurse arrived. The Undertaker came after the Nurse left. The Undertaker was a very strange man. He was even trying to crack some jokes, but he was not even funny. He was 6'5", white, ball headed, and he wore a long black coat. To Christine, he looked creepy. He came, pulled the sheet, slid her mom's body onto the gurney, zipped up the body bag, buckled up the body and left. While he was doing his job, Christine ran into the bedroom, because she couldn't look at her brother when he started crying. But they both decided they wanted to see what was going on. So, they eventually came out of the bedroom. Christine has three brothers and no sisters. Mentally, she was stronger than her brothers and they couldn't handle it. Physically, her brothers were stronger than her. One of Christine's brothers in Florida flew into JFK for the funeral. Her brother, who lives in Trinidad couldn't make it, because he was deported. They never made Funeral Arrangements for anyone. They always hated funerals because they were so scared of dead bodies. But here Christine was sitting and eating next to a dead body. Somehow, God gave them the strength to go through what they had to go through.

They were now making Funeral Arrangements for their mom. Their mom was going to be laid to rest at the Veterans Cemetery next to her husband who was a Veteran. Their mom almost did not make it into the Veterans Cemetery, because they had problems locating their stepfather's plot. Christine's brothers had decided, without her, to burn their mother's body and split the ashes 4 ways. Christine told them that was not going to happen, because she had the Power of Attorney. One of the brothers said to her, "You are pulling rank over us!" We would just have to come up with another plan. Christine was sitting there thinking to herself, what can she do and how was she going to come up with this type of information? Christine quickly called her Spiritual Father, Bishop P, and she told him what was going on. He said, "Don't burn your mother's body. She must be laid to rest in the Veterans Cemetery next to her husband." His wife texted Christine back and asked her his name, the date of his birth and the date he was buried. Christine had very little information to give her and it was a jackpot that this woman of God was able to get the Date and Year he died, and the dates he was in the Nursing Home and the name of the Nursing Home. This was awesome news to Christine that she came up with all the information. The bishop's wife said that she saw a lot of the people who she grew up with listed in the Obituary of the Stepfather. Also, Christine was so happy with the information that this woman, who was up all night, got for her. We had problems locating his burial plot because he was buried under his nickname "CHARLIE" and not his real birth name "CHARLES". But, in the end, everything turned out okay. Christine had prepared herself for her mom's death. She had started to buy certain things that she would like to see her mom dressed in. Christine bought her a tiara for her mom's head, long white silk gloves, a dress which had to be slit in the back, brand new black flat shoes, a fur shawl, pantyhose, underwear, a ring and a bracelet. Her brothers picked out their mom's casket at the Funeral Home and made the necessary arrangements. Christine told the people at the Funeral Home to make her look nice, because her mom only weighed 85 pounds. Christine did not want them to blow her up. Her mom did look fabulous. In the Church that Christine's mom attended, the Pastor said that he didn't want any dead bodies in the Church so Christine decided that she would get a Pastor to do the burial rights at the Funeral Home. One of her Church friends said, "Wow Mary came in with bling and she's leaving with a bling". Christine said, "Yes that's right!"

At the viewing, one of Christine's brothers and his kids came and his kids sat in the back of the Funeral Home, because they had issues with their father because both mother and father were divorced and their mother put them against their father. Christine heard them using bad language in the back of the Funeral Home and not talking to her brother, their father. Christine told her oldest brother that they had to leave, because they were being rude and disrespectful. Eventually, this came out on the Internet, which was very embarrassing. Christine had to remove them from her life until they decided to hear the truth. It was very disgusting, because they weren't kids anymore. They were all in their 20's with deep rooted issues towards their father and Christine's brother. She really didn't understand why people always want to fight at Weddings and Funerals – it's so strange.

Some of the people who knew Christine's mom in her building attended and some wanted too, but they had no transportation. Again, Christine's mom died on December 14, 2016, and she was laid to rest on December 19, 2016, at the Veterans Cemetery. Christine went to Housing and told them what happened, and they already knew. She went there and asked them if they could give her some time to get herself together, they said to her, "I'm very sorry about your mom but you have to get out." Christine asked them if she can live out her mom's rent security? They said, "NO, that money is for the damages to the apartment!" There were no damages to the apartment, because Christine took care of the apartment while she was there.

Christine started to clean out the apartment and threw out some of her mom's things, and some of the people in the building took some. Christine's last brother didn't attend the funeral, because he was deported back home. After the funeral was over, Christine called him and lied to him. She told him that Mammie said, "You must behave yourself." He told his sister, "Yes, Mammie came to him in a dream, and she tried to hug him, and she said to him let us go." He said, he wanted to go with her. But he felt a hand holding him back on his shoulder, he said he couldn't move, because he was stuck. Christine told him the interpretation of the dream was that Mammie came to take him with her, because of him being a constant nuisance and the hand that was holding him back was the hand of God. God was giving him a second chance in life to turn from his wicked ways. If God didn't hold him, he would have died in his sleep. Christine spoke to her brother recently and to her surprise he has changed his ways. Christine guessed that sometimes it takes death to change some people's lives for the better. Christine went to the Building Management where her mom was living, and she asked them to let her stay there for a couple of months until she could get on her feet. One man, said to me "I'm sorry about your mom's death, but you must get out. You don't want to come and find the locks changed?" Again, Christine had to pick up all her strength and courage that she had and head on down to the Agency again. On December 22, 2016, the case worker said to her, "Well since you're still there, there's nothing that they can do for her, so her case was closed. They told Christine to come back in January, in which she did. Christine picked herself up again and went there again on January 3, 2016. Now they can help her, because Christine was now homeless. Christine noticed there was a lot of whispering and pointing. She looked and there was a famous rapper being rushed into the back of the building with bodyguards as big as trees. He came out of a dark-tinted SUV. Christine realized that this famous rapper had child support issues. She also knew who he was, and they also shared the same doctor. Christine was talking to her doctor one day and he told her the same rapper came into his office and passed through the back door with huge bodyguards as big as trees and all the nurses in the office were asking him for his autograph. The doctor said he called all the nurses in the office and warned them to leave this rapper alone. The doctor didn't know who he was, and he had to go home and ask his son who he was, and the doctor told Christine his son pulled up a video with the rapper and that's when he realized who he was. While Christine waited for her number to be called so that she could be interviewed by a Case Worker; while Christine was sitting there, she overheard a Spanish Woman say, "I hate Homeless Shelters, I'm at my wit's end, I can't take it anymore, I'm going crazy." Christine was scared and she said to her case worker that she didn't want to go to a Shelter, and she asked to be put into a hotel. The case worker said to her, "Miss that's all we have, and you must go where we place you; unless you have somewhere you can stay or somebody who will take you in." Christine said, "Okay." Christine was on her way to a Homeless Shelter on Long Island and she was told that you were only allowed one bag when she got there. Christine was expecting a big building. It was a neat house along with other homeowners on each side. She was given the rules of the Shelter. Christine had options to go back to Florida and stay with her brother until she got back on her feet. Christine told him, "No" and that she would stay in New York. If Christine had left New York and gone to Florida, she would not have met all these characters in the Homeless Shelter and you who are reading this book would not have loved it. HA-HA!!

NOW CHRISTINE IS OFFICIALLY HOMELESS AND LIVING IN A SHELTER FOR WOMEN

The rules were:

NO DRUGS WHATSOEVER.

NO TALKING ON THE PHONE DURING LIGHTS OUT.

NO DIRTY CLOTHES AND NO CURSING.

NO FIGHTING.

NO VISITORS.

NO BORROWING ITEMS.

NO LOUD MUSIC.

NO WEAPONS OF ANY SORT.

NO ALCOHOLIC BEVERAGES.

NO UNAUTHORIZED PRESCRIPTION MEDICATION.

NO PARAPHERNALIA ALLOWED ON THE PREMISES.

NO GAMBLING.

NO TALKING WHILE YOU ARE ON THE BUFFET LINE FOR LUNCH OR DINNER.

NO REACHING OVER SOMEONE ELSE'S PLATE OR CUP.

ALWAYS TURN OFF THE LIGHTS IN THE KITCHEN AND BATHROOM.

IF THE WEATHER IS 30 DEGREES OUTSIDE, YOU ARE ALLOWED TO STAY IN.

THE ONLY BEVERAGE ALLOWED IN THE ROOM IS ONLY WATER AND PEPPERMINT CANDY.

CLEAN UP AFTER YOURSELF IN THE KITCHEN AND ROOM.

YOU ARE ONLY ALLOWED 2 SPOONS OF SUGER FOR YOUR TEA.

YOU'RE NOT ALLOWED TO DRINK THE STAFF COFFEE.

YOU'RE NOT ALLOWED TO GO INTO THE STAFF PANTRY.

SHOWERS MUST BE TAKEN AT 6:30 AM TO 8:30 AM.

YOU MUST BE OUT BY 9:30 AM IN THE MORNING.

EVERYONE HAS 15 MINUTES IN THE BATHROOM.

NO DOING LAUNDRY ON THE PREMISES (LAUNDROMAT).

YOU ARE NOT ALLOWED TO BRING IN FOOD FROM THE OUTSIDE (EXCEPT ON THURSDAYS, FRIDAYS, AND SATURDAYS) EVERYTHING THAT'S LEFT WILL BE THROWN OUT ON SUNDAYS.

THERE'S A CURFEW THAT YOU MUST BE IN
BY 9 PM FROM MONDAY TO FRIDAY AND ON
SATURDAYS, THE CURFEW IS UNTIL 12:30
MIDNIGHT.

THE FOOD IS TERRIBLE IN THIS SHELTER. I
CAN'T SPEAK FOR OTHER SHELTERS, BUT IN
THIS PARTICULAR SHELTER, IT IS TERRIBLE.

What Christine didn't realize was that God allowed her
to go into the Shelter to minister to some of these women in the
Shelter, and Christine also inspired two of these women to go
and get their license to work as Nurse's Aides. One of whom did
receive their Certificate and the other didn't get her Certificate,
because she missed days, and the teacher told her that she missed
too many days from school and that she would have to start
over again and she refused. In the Shelter, they put everyone
together. Some people had psychological problems, some have
drug problems and the rest like Christine were normal.

Christine quickly realized why the Spanish woman at the
Agency was complaining, because there are too many rules and
regulations and not many people can follow rules. Most of them,
don't like the Shelter. The reason for that is that they cannot
sleep late, party like a rock star, and they can't have their man or
their woman laying up in the Women's Shelter with them.

Christine was given one roll of toilet paper, and she had
to sign the papers and abide by the rules and regulations of the
Shelter. Christine came in cold, hungry, and tired. She was given
white rice and fried chicken to eat. She scoffed it down and the
next day, Christine had diarrhea. She was told that the food was

there for four days, and it was being heated repeatedly.

A couple of days after that, Christine was served a dinner box of macaroni and cheese, frozen vegetables, and a hamburger. The hamburger was baked, it was so hard, and it had no seasoning; it was black and hard as a hockey puck. One of Christine's roommates couldn't eat the hamburger. Poor Rose Mary had no teeth, and she had tried to bite it, but the hamburger won. She put it back on her plate and Christine just looked at her and laughed.

Christine also noticed that some of these women in the Shelter had drug problems and psychological problems and they didn't care. She would ask, "What happened and why are you here?" They would say things like; "I was in jail, or I didn't get along with my mom, or I lost my apartment." To some of them, it was like a revolving door.

One young woman they found passed out on Campus grounds at 2:00 am and the Police Officer took her and brought her to the Shelter. She was up the next morning asking for toiletries.

Christine gave her some toothpaste. She took a shower, and we never saw or heard from her again.

There are people and different organizations who stop by and drop off things for the women in the Shelter that Christine was in but some of the Counselors took what they wanted and stored the rest in the Pantry downstairs. Someone took out a frozen turkey and the turkey was left on the dish rack for five days then it was cooked. Christine refused to eat that baked turkey. Christine learned quickly.

The next day, one of the Counselors who goes by the name of JESSIE was once a resident there. Also, she was a drug dealer, and she is now married to her husband who is a woman. Yes, her husband who she gets on the phone and talks to any old way she chooses too. JESSIE is clean and sober now and she works as a counselor. Christine laid on the top bunk bed and JESSIE shouted from the top of her lungs, "Dinner"! Christine was shocked. Christine asked, "Who is that and why is she shouting like that?" The other women said it was dinner time. Christine was hungry so she got off her bunk bed and went to get her dinner. Christine should have stayed in her bed. What was served was burnt pizza. Now, who burns frozen pizza? JESSIE does and JESSIE has the nerve to say you are only allowed two slices of pizza. We were all hungry, so we had to endure the burnt pizza. You couldn't tell the pepperoni from the cheese. You had to eat it or starve. No one starved that day. JESSIE said she can't cook and it's true. Who burns a frozen pizza?

Christine was the new person. There are three people in one room with a bunk bed and a single bed. Guess who was on top of the bunk bed? Christine made friends with all the ladies in her room quickly. She was quickly learning and taking every piece of information that was given to her by these women. Most of the women in the Shelter were very helpful to Christine, they gave her the information that she needed, and they also helped her with what she didn't know and what she needed to know. Again, she knew it was God's plan for her to be there. Now that Christine completed the assignment that God had given her regarding her mom, she was on to the next assignment. Although Christine was in a Shelter, she picked herself up and started going back to Church. Some Church members knew what happened and they knew where Christine was staying. So, they prayed for her and encouraged her. Christine needed the encouragement.

Some of the Counselors and workers in the Shelter were once residents of the Shelter. So, it was nice to see and hear how they fought their way out of the Shelter. Christine also realized the way the System is set up that if you don't fight and claw your way to get out of the Shelter, you will continue to bounce from Shelter to Shelter, because some of the women that Christine encountered, have been there for months and years. She knew that she was going to leave, so she decided to make the best of her life in the Shelter while she was residing there.

Most of the people have relatives that live right in the area and are homeowners. But they refuse to take them in, because of their mouth and that they have no respect or regard for other people.

Christine soon realized that different agencies would help you as much as possible to get you back on your feet. For example, if you need an address, you can use their address to get your mail, if you're an American or American Citizen, they'll help you obtain your birth certificate for $50.00. If you need your resume done, there are places that you can go to type up your resume. If you need clothes for a job interview and they will send you to a place where you can get an outfit. If you need a bath, they will help you, and if you need food, you can come and eat there. The food was good, and the servers were friendly and respectable.

THE NAMES OF THESE WOMEN WERE MADE UP IN ORDER TO PROTECT THEIR IDENTITIES.

LIFE IN THE SHELTER AND THE CHARACTERS IN THE SHELTER

THEY ARE REAL PEOPLE

MRS. BROWN

There was this black woman who was heavy set, and her name was Mrs. Brown. Christine asked Mrs. Brown, "What happened and why did she end up there in the Shelter?" Her story made Christine's hair on her arms and on the back of her neck stand straight up. At that time, Mrs. Brown and her husband who was a trucker lived directly across the Street from the Shelter. Mrs. Brown's husband got shot and died, so she ended up in the Shelter by not being able to pay her rent and the rest of the bills. She got evicted and had no place to stay and she ended up directly across the street from where she and her deceased husband use to live. Mrs. Brown said, she made the necessary funeral arrangements from the money she received from Mr. Brown's family. She dressed the part of a grieving widow in black from head to toe including the black veil. At the Funeral, Mrs. Brown quickly realized she was not the only Mrs. Brown. There were two other Mrs. Browns. It seems the husband was the truck driver, and he married two other women in different States and failed to tell Mrs. Brown who was wife number three and that he had two other wives. No, Mr. Brown was not a Muslim. Now, Wife number three and number two started fighting at the funeral throwing fists, kicking, punching, scratching, biting, and tearing each other's weave and clothes off; while wife number one, who's the original wife, looked on. Well needless to say, wife number one, who's the original wife, ended up with all the benefits. So, this is why wife number three ended up in the Shelter bitter, rude, stressed out, broken, and mean. Eventually, she moved out and moved on with her life with a hatred for all men. Mrs. Brown eventually turned to women.

SHARON

Sharon was a Haitian woman. She was in the Shelter for a couple of months. I was told she came out of prison after spending 25 years in prison for burning her Italian husband to death while he slept on the couch. Everyone feared her. Sharon was educated and her husband wanted out of the relationship, and she wasn't having it. So, Sharon planned to commit murder-suicide, but when the flames hit, Sharon took the baby, jumped through the window and escaped leaving her husband to die. At the trial, she tried to claim insanity, but the jury did not buy her insanity act, so she was sentenced to 25 years in prison.

LISA

There was Lisa, a Jamaican married woman, with a teenage daughter and with a husband who physically abused her. So, she started drinking to cope. Lisa became an alcoholic, and she said her grandfather was an alcoholic, and he died from it. Lisa ended up in the Shelter. She would drink so much that she would black out anywhere she was, and men and women would take advantage of her. Her daughter lived with Lisa's sister who was her aunt. Once Lisa entered the Shelter, there were rules she had to abide by. Lisa's drinking got worse. When Lisa got drunk, she would curse everybody out and wanted to fight. She was a mean drunk. When she was sober, people showed her videos of her behavior. She couldn't believe it. Lisa was kicked out of the Shelter by one of the Counselors who would make sure that she went to her room and slept. Lisa cursed out the Counselor. Lisa also attended AAA. But it didn't seem to help her. The last thing I heard was that Lisa was transferred to a Women's Shelter in Suffolk County.

LAVINIA

There is a young lady by the name of Lavinia, a bi-racial woman. Lavinia is a sweet young woman who is very naive. If she is not careful, the world and all the users will eat her up and spit her out. She stands 6'3" tall and wore a size 14 in shoes. Christine asked her, "What happened and why was she in the Shelter?" Lavinia said her mother, who was white, died of Stage Four Cancer of the Uterus. Her mom did everything for her and the rest of the family. Her Dad, a retired Police Officer, who was black, called the cops and put her out of the house. Lavinia's brother would beat her up and blame her for the death of their mother. Lavinia had another brother who died in prison. He had many health issues, and he was taken to one of the Hospitals near the prison and he died. Lavinia's father, who is a retired police officer, fears the son, and he is lost, confused, and doesn't know what to do, so he decided to put his only daughter out of the house. Lavinia needs to be in a Shelter for Battered Women. Christine then asked her, if she had any aunts, uncles, or grandparents with whom she could stay. She said, they didn't want any part of her, because she is not of their heritage. Christine figured that if Lavinia stood 6'3" tall then her brother must be taller and stronger than Lavinia. Lavinia needed a lot of help, and she had a boyfriend, who she was staying with the and boyfriend went to jail. The boyfriend's parents told her she had to leave. Christine was walking down the street one day and from a distance, she saw this very tall very fair-skinned young lady sitting on the side of the road. As Christine got closer, it was Lavinia. Christine asked her what she was doing there and why she was sitting at the side of the road. "She said that she was making a phone call." Christine said to her, "You don't have to sit at the side of the road on your cell phone making calls." She told her that she looked like a hooker. When Christine looked up, there were men in cars already circling the block checking her out. So, Christine said to her, "Get up and let's go to the library where's it warm and you can charge your phone and talk quietly on your phone. "She agreed. While the two of them walked and they talked, Lavinia finally got enrolled at a Community College. Christine knows Lavinia and her whole family need counseling. She stated she still sees her dad and they meet at a Coffee Shop to have coffee and talk. Christine knows Lavinia still loves her dad very much and her dad loves her too. Last night, she had a toothache. She called her dad, and he came and got her, and they went and bought the medication she needed for the toothache. She still has lots of things to work out. All who are in the Shelter had to be out by 10:00 am and Lavinia sleeps until 10:15 am The Counselors must bang on the door and tell her to get out. Lavinia said they were mean to her and Christine told her that they were not mean to her. You're not following the rules, and she told her to set her phone alarm for 8:00 am so that she could have enough time to get up and get herself together. She said, "she didn't think of that." Well, Christine told her that while she is in the Shelter, she will help her as much as she can. She is so lost and should be in a Battered Shelter for Women so that she can get the necessary counseling that she needs and so that she can move on in her life. Christine and Lavinia ran into each other again, just as Christine was getting ready to leave to go outside. As she stated earlier, you must be out by 10:00 am. Lavinia was just coming downstairs at 10:00 am to take a shower when she knew very well that she had to be out by 10:00. Christine figured out that some people you try to reach are unreachable. Lavinia made me proud since she decided to go back to school and take a course in Nursing. Lavinia missed one day of class and the instructor told her that she had to start the course over, because she had missed too much information. Lavinia was also studying to become a Firefighter. Of course, she didn't complete her Nursing studies. I'm happy to say that Christine had inspired Lavinia to go back to school and take a course in Nursing. Christine hopes that Lavinia do decides to go back and take the Nursing Course. Christine again ran into Lavinia, and she's taken the test for the Fire Department.

REESE

Then there was a young lady whose name was Reese, and she was 37 years old with four children. She said one of her daughters' fathers is Guyanese. She came in on a Sunday and we started talking.

She asked me how the Counselors are there during the week. She told her they were okay and there were just rules that you must follow. She started to cry saying that she had a hard time following rules and that she had physiological problems, and she went to see a Counselor. Reese didn't care about rules. She wanted to do what she wanted to do no matter who said what to her. Reese was also picky, and she didn't eat this and didn't eat that. She wanted to go out and buy her own food and that did not sit well with the Counselors. The Shelter that she was staying in before, she came to the Shelter where she was staying, and she got herself kicked out. Christine asked her where she was before she got kicked out of the other Shelter. She said that she was in jail and was there for three years, and that she got married to a woman in there and that woman is still locked up. By Reese's attitude, Christine knew there was going to be trouble right from the start. On Monday Reese started acting out. She came in high, ran up the stairs and was disoriented. She then came down from upstairs with her pants and underwear down to her knees and she went and sat on the toilet bowl with the door wide open crying hysterically and out of it. She got out of the bathroom and walked around with her pants and underwear down to her knees. Her other roommates were so scared, shocked, and in disbelief that they were shaking. Christine guessed that they had never seen anyone behave the way she did. The Counselor told her to pull her pants and underwear up, because she you can't walk around the Shelter like that, and she had to respect the other women. That did not sit too well with her. She ran upstairs again and started banging on the door. Then she ran outside in the rain and left. The Counselor told her that she was not going to put up with her mess. The Counselor got up and went upstairs, packed her belongings and what fell out of her bag was a DILDO. The Counselor said to her "Where's 24 the respect for roommates?" The Counselor took her belongings and placed them outside in the rain. Christine felt bad for her when the Counselor placed her things like that outside in the rain. Well, Reese came back banging and kicking the door, she used her cell phone to knock on the window. The Counselor did not let her in, but instead, the Counselor called 911 and they came in a flash. She wanted her juice in the refrigerator, and it was given to her, and she left. You would think that was the end of the story. Not by a long shot, Reese came back again kicking the door, trying to punch the Counselor. Reese said, "You'll a bunch of ghetto people in there." She wanted her money and her things. This time the cops came, and they put the handcuffs on her and she was crying, kicking, and screaming. Reese was given a nice warm bed in the Psychiatric Ward. Christine knew the neighbors were watching. Christine had never seen anything like it before and so did the rest of the people in the Shelter who were shocked and shaken up. They could not believe this was happening on a rainy Monday afternoon. Reese is in another facility now.

ROSE

Then there is Rose, who is in her late 80s. An old white German woman who's in the Shelter and she's one of Christine's roommates. Christine asked her, "Why was she in a Shelter?" Rose and her family lived in a beautiful 5-bedroom house in Long Island. All the family died, and the house was left to Rose in a Will. Rose didn't pay her taxes when she lived with the family. The family did everything. After Rose's Aunt died, the house was given to her and Rose's beautiful home went into foreclosure. The Sheriff came and told her that she had to get out and Rose just grabbed a couple of things and left everything behind. Rose roamed the streets for one year pushing a shopping cart until she ended up in the Shelter. Christine asked her if she had any family members who she could go and live with. Rose's father was a Chef, and her mother worked in the Hospital in the Cafeteria. She said she had a brother who died and a niece who died when she was 13 years old. Christine was glad the Counselors who were there looked out for her and took care of her. They would remind her to take her medication. As stated before, during the week you must be out by 10:00 am and you can come back by 3:00 pm. If it goes below 30 degrees, you get to stay in. Rose does not leave the Shelter. Rose only leaves the Shelter just to go to her appointments or to go outside and look at the cat in the back of the house. She gets her meals from an Agency; she has a Counselor who takes her to the Agency when she must go to be recertified. One day Christine asked Rose, "Why don't you sign up for a Senior Citizen Building?" Rose said to Christine, "Why you don't go?" Christine laughed, because she couldn't believe what she had said to her. Christine didn't let it bother her, because she was old. Christine told her,

"You'll have your very own apartment, and you can interact with people your age and there are lots of activities for you to do." In the Senior Citizen Buildings, they take you to plays, restaurants, movies, baseball games, and the Casino to gamble. Christine knows because her mom lived in the Senior Citizen Building as she stated in the earlier pages. Christine's Mom did say that those people in the Senior Citizen Building were nosy, and they mind people's business. Christine would laugh. Well as for Rose, she's funny and she's quite happy staying where she is. No   Christine guessed that's what keeps her going and she's happy there. Having Rose as a roommate, the TV must be shut off by 9:00 pm and in the morning the TV goes on at 7:00 am. Christine didn't mind really; Rose led an interesting life when she was young. The Lord put it into my spirit to go to the Pantry where they give out clothes and Christine went and got some things for Rose. Christine got her two sweaters, a designer bag, a comforter blanket, a bar of soap, an address book, a pack of pampers for the elderly, a big bath towel, and matching gloves and scarfs. She gave them to Rose, and she picked out what she wanted. The designer bag she didn't want. Rose claimed it was too small; the comforter blanket was too big for her and the pampers for the elderly, Rose said, "I don't want it, and you can't make me wear it." Christine just laughed. Rose reminds her of her mom, because Christine's mom was the same way too. But eventually, she had to wear them. Rose is still Rose. She is a strong, stubborn, and a very independent woman. Christine is praying for Rose to move into a Senior Citizen Building so that she can get the help that she needs. As for Rose, she is set in her ways and she's very stubborn. Her Counselor found her a Senior Citizen Building and she was told that she had to fill out the form and give them the information regarding her Bank

Account and that didn't sit too well with Rose. She said, "That's my money and it stays in my Account. I'm not going, and they can't make me go." Again, an attorney came to visit Rose in the Shelter, the attorney wanted her to sign some papers so they could put her in a better Facility, and she said, "No" that she was not going and the attorney got mad. They had to call the owner of the place, and they gave Rose the phone and after the Director spoke with her, she signed the papers. Rose is thinking that she can move into a Nursing Home for free and keep all her money in the bank. What's going to happen to Rose is that from there they'll put her in a Nursing Home. Because her health is failing and she is a very frail person and she's very stubborn. Rose is still at the Shelter. Christine ran into some of her old friends who were at the Shelter, and she asked what happened to Rose? They said, "Rose had to move into a Senior Citizen Building where she is being taken care of."

MARTHA

Then there is MARTHA. She is a white woman in her 50s. Martha has some kind of stomach problem, and she relies on some type of painkiller medication. If you have any medical condition, the Counselors will take your medication and give you the medication when you need it. They didn't want anybody who has a drug problem to help themselves with your prescription. Well, this Counselor took Martha's medication and left it on the table and in a split second, someone helped themselves to Martha's medication. It was one of the other roommates in the other room who helped herself to Martha's prescription. Martha went to the doctor trying to get more. Of course, they didn't give Martha any more pain killers. My dear friend Martha was in such pain, and she ended up in the Hospital. They believe she sold it, and they didn't believe the medication was stolen. The doctor sent an affidavit for Martha and the Counselor to sign, then there were police reports to be filled out and this case ended up in Court, because Martha took them to Court for not giving her more medication. It was one big confusion. The Counselor who didn't put away the medication was fired for leaving the medication on the table instead of locking up the medication. Well, they finally found out who took Martha's medication. The woman who took Martha's medication, her name is Chrystal. Chrystal has two kids and she's always in and out of jail and bouncing in and out of different Shelters. She stated that she's not going back to jail, and she said, "She would rather die!" I guess thug life was too hard for her. Chrystal was kicked out of the Shelter and while she was out in the streets, she found a room. One of her sons, who was a teenager, was not seeing or hearing from his mother, so he decided to go and visit his mom.

When he got there, Chrystal was dead. She had been dead for a couple of days. She had overdosed on some type of drugs. RIP Chrystal.

CAROLYN

Then there was Carolyn. Carolyn was married and divorced with two sons. She also lived with her dad in a Senior Citizen Building, and she took care of him until the time of his death.

Again, Carolyn, Victoria, and I had similar situations. Carolyn's Dad gave her $300,000.00 Carolyn didn't invest her money well at all. How can someone run through $300,000.00 and have nothing to show for it? She used up her money by partying like a rock star, taking trips, buying expensive dinners, clothes, jewelry, and fancy cars. Now Carolyn is an alcoholic and living in a Shelter. Carolyn hit rock bottom very fast and hard. Her ex-husband had her kids, and she was sleeping on the street on a cardboard box where people were taking advantage of her while she laid passed out high on the street. It took her a while to get herself together. Her sons would put her up in hotels for a night trying to help her. But Carolyn got her act together herself. She's going to meetings at least 3 to 5 times a week for her addiction. She's helpful and kind. But Christine suspects she is still taking some type of drugs. When she looks at her while she is speaking, Christine can see that she's shaking slightly. If she's still using, she's only fooling herself. Carolyn said they gave her some type of drugs to take, and she said, "It's very strong and if you take a drink, you can get very sick." Christine cannot mention the name of the drug, because of legal reasons. Christine knows most drug users are in denial, and they know every trick in the book. One of the Counselors told Christine that they sometimes come into the Shelter with the bottle of alcohol under their coats or they put it at the bottom of their handbag. They're not fooling anyone, but themselves. Slowly, she's coming around. She said her son said that she could come and live with him when she is ready. Christine told her to stay strong and continue to go to her meetings and stay away from bad company. She said she knew. Christine does hope that Carolyn makes it out of the Shelter. Christine ran into Carolyn, and she looked great. They just moved her to another Shelter out in Suffolk County.

VICTORIA

Then there is Victoria. Victoria is a black woman with big hips. She was born in Germany and she's arguing with Christine telling Christine she's an American. Christine told her that you were born in Germany and you are German. She told me she has Dual Citizenship. She said she left Germany when she was a little girl, and she can only count from 1 to 10. Christine told her that she is a German. Victoria and Christine had a similar situation. She too took care of her mom who died of cancer, and she lived with her mom and when her mom died, they put her out. Because just like Christine, her mom lived in a Senior Citizen Building. Well, back to my story about Victoria. She had eight kids, four boys and two girls. Two of her oldest kids died from being shot by the Police. Victoria sued the city, and she was awarded a settlement of 2.5 million dollars. She is married and her husband is in jail serving nine years. Victoria squandered her money on trips, jewelry, and brand clothes and she ended up on drugs roaming the streets. Victoria was being bounced from Shelter to Shelter all up and down Long Island. She started going to Church, but she still had one foot in the Church and one foot in the streets. The Pastor of the Church, where she would attend, would drive by while she was roaming the streets and ask her, "Where you were going?" She replied, "I'm going up the street." Well, God had a calling on her life and this time she was not going to get away. That very same day, Victoria went to Church, and she ran straight to the altar and threw herself down and she passed out. God got her good. Victoria said her kids told her that she could come and stay with them. Victoria did not want to stay with her children, because she said that they'll make her a built-in babysitter. She said, "She wanted to do this on her own." Now, the streets are history. Victoria is now a born-again Christian. She met a Muslim guy and they've been living together for nine years. Who knows, the Holy Spirit got a hold of her to stop living together and to get married. The intimacy in the relationship ceased, so they got engaged. The Muslim fiancé thought that if he gave her an engagement ring, he would be getting some sex from Victoria, but "No," Victoria was not having it. One day Victoria said, "Let's go into the city since it is a Holiday," Christine said, "Okay" since she was not doing anything, so they agreed to go. They went up to Harlem where they met her Muslim fiancé. Over the phone, they took some vows which she called it the Shahada. Christine realized quickly she was being used as a witness. Victoria was ready to marry her Muslim boyfriend right there and then. Victoria thought since her fiancé□ was Muslim and she was a Christian that she didn't have to get a divorce from her husband in jail and that the rules didn't apply to her or him. She was speaking to someone on the phone from the Muslim Faith and they told her that she must get a divorce from her husband in jail and then they can get married. If they did get married now, they both can go to jail for bigamy. The wedding is put on hold for now until she gets a divorce from her husband. Victoria is Christine's bunk buddy. Christine slept on the top and Victoria slept on the bunk below. She attends Church regularly and she even invited Christine to Church. Christine saw a change in her, and she was much happier. But there will be a struggle between her fiancé□ and her. He's already dictating to her telling her all Muslim women's heads must remain covered. Victoria sees she's already changing her ways to please him. Christine will just sit back and observe. Last night, Victoria was crying and Christine asked her why she was crying, and she said, "She wants her

Mammie, and she misses her Mammie." Christine had to go and sit next to her and console her. Christine told her that they were both in the same boat. She lost her mom too and Christine told her that both of their moms were watching over them. Christine felt very bad for her, because she misses her mom too. I guess you're never too old to miss your mom, because she was crying. Christine had to get up and get her glass of water to drink. Well, Victoria is already taking the steps to divorce her husband so she can marry her Muslim Fiancé□ . Well, Victoria got a 3-bedroom apartment. So, as she waits for the apartment to be fixed up, soon she can move out of the Shelter. I'm glad for her, because she's been bouncing around for seven long months. Now, all Victoria must do is to get out of the Women's Shelter. The apartment for Victoria fell through. The owner did not want to rent to someone who had children, because the tenant before her, the woman allowed her children to tear up the woman's apartment and the owner had to take money out of her pocket to repair the damages. So, Victoria is still in the Shelter and still is trying. One morning around 7:30 am, there was a knock on the door and there were eight detectives who came in with search warrants, and they had on bulletproof vests with their guns drawn. Some came to the front of the door, and some came to the back of the door. They were looking for Victoria's daughter. Victoria's daughter is 18 years old, and her name is Keisha. She is supposed to be with her mother. But she decided to stay with her no-good boyfriend and the two of them were sleeping in abandoned buildings, and doorways. Well, Christine never experienced anything like that before and she was so scared. Christine was in the shower and when she came out of the shower, there were tall men with guns and bulletproof vests on. They came with two unmarked vehicles, and they were ready for war. Victoria's daughter was not on the premises. The detectives asked Victoria where her daughter was, and she said she didn't know. The detectives left, but Christine knew she knew her daughter's whereabouts. Two weeks after that, the Detectives came back again looking for Victoria's daughter. Victoria said, she didn't know where her daughter was. The detective took her aside and they told her that if she didn't start helping them, that they were going to start coming after every family member. Victoria left and contacted her daughter. After that incident, she didn't say much. Christine went to work and when she returned from work, Victoria informed us that her daughter was in the Hospital with a kidney infection. Now, she wants her daughter to stay with her in the Shelter. Let's see how this will work. Victoria also has psychological problems, and she got up one night to use the bathroom and then she was sitting on her bed in the dark. Christine asked her if she was ok, and she said, yes. Christine also inspired Victoria, and she decided to go back to school and take a course in nursing. Christine is so proud of herself for inspiring both Lavinia & Victoria. Victoria's daughter did come and stay with us in the Shelter after they picked up her daughter's boyfriend. He had many warrants out on him, and they picked him up early one morning coming out of a Motel. He was arrested right on the spot. Victoria's daughter vowed to stay by her boyfriend's side to the end. She's 18 years old and that's not going to happen. Victoria's daughter stayed with us and that didn't last too long. She lasted a week, and they put her out, because she's 18 years old and she couldn't abide by the rules. Victoria's daughter is a prostitute, and everyone has tried talking her out of it. She said, "It's my job and no one can stop me." At least, she gave it a try. Christine ran into Victoria, and she was selling loose cigarettes at the Bus Terminal. The Security Guards chased her out of the Bus Terminal. Christine again, ran into Victoria and this time, she was taking care of a patient who lived near Christine. Victoria moved to another Shelter and she's depending on Social Services. Christine ran into Victoria again she finally got an apartment and she's doing okay. Christine went and took a Healthcare Course and Victoria followed Christine also because she was inspired by her.

CARMEN

Then there was Carmen who lives in the Shelter with us. When Christine arrived, she was there. Carmen is a white middle-aged female in her late 50's and she worked in Corporate for many years on Wall Street. She lost her job, her marriage fell apart, and her kids wouldn't speak to her for whatever reason. So, Carmen ended up on drugs and became homeless. Carmen has a twin brother from what we were told. Carmen is very educated, and she is also a web designer. At the Shelter, breakfast is served from 7:00 a.m. to 9:00 a.m. Then we must leave at 10:00 am. Carmen goes to all the fast-food restaurants and stands next to the drive-thru area. When any car passes and they drop any change, and they refuse to get out of their car to pick up the change from the ground, Carmen goes and picks up the loose change. I asked Carmen what was going on and she told me that she needed a cup of coffee to drink. I asked her did she drink coffee at the Shelter and if she knew that there was a Food Pantry about four blocks away from where they lived in which she could get all the food, coffee, tea, and water. She refused to answer. Christine didn't know what Carmen's no response to her questions all was about. Carmen also has heart disease, high cholesterol, diabetes and she's an alcoholic. She works as a file clerk, and she complains that they're underpaying her. Christine told her it was better than not having a job at all. Carmen was kicked out of the Shelter where she was staying, because she was caught drinking alcohol on the premises. So, she was sent to another Shelter. We heard from a friend that Carmen was kicked out of that Shelter also, because she was caught drinking again. So, they placed her somewhere out in

East Suffolk County. Christine didn't know what happened to Carmen.

SHAKIRA

Then there is Shakira. She is a tall, big black woman, straight from jail and they placed her in the Women's Shelter. Shakira had all her kids taken away from her. She had a bad attitude.

She's mad at the world and I guess she misses her kids. Shakira has gotten into arguments with about four of the women already. We know that she won't be here much longer. We all try to get along and help each other out. But, not Shakira. She has this attitude like the world owes her something. If you sit too close to her, she'll complain, don't stand next to her or empty a plate when dinner is being served, she'll tell you don't lean over her plate. Her roommates are walking on eggshells whenever she's around. One of her roommates, who stays with her in her room, stands up to her. Christine loves that she will not be bullied. Because of Shakira, Lavinia was out in the hallway crying and she was so scared of Shakira when she said she would smack her in the face. Lavinia told the Counselors, and they warned her. On a cold Sunday morning, 16 degrees outside, Shakira got into an argument with another woman and the cops were called, and she was escorted off the property. That was the end of Shakira. Christine sees her sometimes, but they are not friends, so they pass each other, and they do not even say Hi or Hello.

JENN

Then there is Jenn. She's a black woman in her late 40's. Jenn is very educated and very athletic in sports. She had a couple of scholarships to attend different colleges. Jenn had a good life. Both her mother and father were separated, so Jenn stayed with her dad. Jenn was always surrounded by lots of family members and lots of cousins her age while growing up. She had whatever she wanted, and she didn't lack anything. When the drug problem started, prayers were being done on her behalf. Many people would talk to her and all that talking went in one ear and came out the other ear. Jenn fell into the wrong crowd. Jenn had five boys, and the last boy, she placed with her family and the family saw that no money was coming their way, so they told her to come and get the little boy, or they will call the Agency. Jenn decided she was going to enter a drug rehab facility. It was not the first rehab that didn't last long, because she was out on the street again. Her kids were taken away from her. Jenn's life was spiraling out of control very fast. Jen would lay passed out in the streets, abandoned buildings, bars, and sidewalks. She eventually picked up many diseases. Jenn was HIV positive and then AIDS. Jenn was not taking any medication, and she was still running the street. Eventually, the disease won, and Jenn was too far gone for any medication to work. Again, the disease won. Jenn died and her kids grew up and I'm very proud to say that none of her children ever did drugs. They are today all working; they have their businesses, and Jenn did not live to see her beautiful grandchildren. Jenn was buried by her little sister Lola. Lola dressed her big sister like a princess. REST IN PARADISE.

SHARON

Then there is Sharon a white woman in her late 60s. We were having breakfast one morning and we asked her why she was in the Shelter? We were all afraid to ask her because she had a mean look on her face. Sharon would always come downstairs for breakfast dressed nicely. She's quiet and she keeps to herself. When they asked, what happened and why she was in the Shelter? It seemed like she wanted to let loose her mouth as it was just flowing. Sharon said she went to the eye doctor for a checkup and one of the machines stuck her in the eye and she fell and hit her head, and she laid unconscious. Christine asked her if she had taken legal action, and she said, "No." Christine said to her, "Why not?" She said, she didn't know, because it happened 10 years ago." She said at that time; she and her husband were getting ready to go to Florida, because her husband was offered a better-paying job. The job didn't work out for her husband, so they're divorced, and her daughter lives with her ex-husband. Sharon stated that she was on her own from the time she was 18. What does this have to do with not filing a lawsuit? To make matters worse, Sharon was hit by a truck while she was driving, and her daughter was in the car with her. Again, no lawsuit. This happened about 5 years ago. Christine gave her the phone number of an attorney who worked for the same company with her for over 20 years. Eventually, Sharon and her husband are divorced. The daughter lives with her father and Sharon is in the Shelter like a lost soul. Sometimes you don't know what people are going through. Christine realized that she wanted someone to talk to, so she gave her the number of a good attorney and it's up to her to put this number to good use. Christine told Sharon she was sitting on a big pile of money. By talking to Sharon, I realized she's a very nice lady who keeps to herself, minds her business and goes about her business. Christine recently spoke to Sharon, and she told her that she was moving out and she got an apartment on Long Island. We were all happy for her. It was nice knowing her.

TINA

Tina came into the Shelter one night. It was cold and dark. The next day, Tina started acting out. We could tell from the get-go that she would not be a good fit. Tina kept saying, "I want to go to a hotel." The hotels have no rules. You can sleep as late as you want, eat when you want, and you can come and go as you please. No one tells you anything. Well, if they gave out awards for people who fake mental illness, Tina would receive the highest award. Tina started complaining about being nervous and she can't stand being around a lot of people. Tina started shaking, she threw herself on the ground and started shaking, rolling, spitting, and kicking. While she is putting on the best performance of her life, the Counselors called 911. Christine was told that once you go to the Hospital, they put on the band on your risk to show the ID that you were in the Hospital, and that something was wrong with you. The Counselors called the Ambulance, and they came in a matter of minutes and took Tina to the Hospital. The next day, one of the Counselors saw Tina at the Agency shaking and spitting, and of course, she had the bracelet ID from the Hospital which is what she wanted so that she could go to a hotel. The Agency read the report, and they placed her in the hotel which is where she wanted to go. Then Tina's boyfriend was also staying in a Homeless Shelter for men. She gave him a call and he left the Shelter and joined Tina in the hotel where they could be together and do as they pleased. Well, Tina deserved the highest award for best performance ever.

MS. BEATRICE

Ms. B is a very vibrant old Jamaican woman in her late 70s. She had five kids and many grandchildren. She's been in the Shelter for two and one half and years. Ms. B, as everyone calls her, you can tell that back in the day, she was a very stylish woman with her clothes and hats always matching and as for her age, she's not taking crap from anyone. From what was told Ms. B was living with her daughter, who is an owner of a Real Estate Agency in Long Island. Ms. B wanted to run her daughter's household and her grandchildren's life. This brought bad blood between the rest of the adult children. So, her daughter put her out and the other daughter told Ms. B to come to Florida and that didn't work out either. Ms. B said, "She and her daughter couldn't get along either." Both daughters put her out and that's how she ended up in the Shelter and this is where she is right now. Some mothers and fathers must know when to shut their faces, because you can't be in your children's business all the time. Again, Ms. B is a very vibrant woman, and she goes to the Senior Citizen Center. She does her Zumba dancing, yoga, and exercise. She's a funny lady that when she speaks, she makes you laugh. Ms. B got into it with Shakira who just came out of jail. Shakira called Ms. B a stupid Bitch which got Ms. B very upset, and she got up ready to fight with Shakira. Need I remind you that Ms. B has a bad heart and knee problems. They had to hold Ms. B back as the two of them were getting ready to go at each other. Once Ms. B gets on her phone, she gossips for hours about her family members. Again, some parents need to shut their mouths. Ms. B often cooked her food. Once she was boiling an egg in the microwave and the egg exploded, and she suffered burns all over her arms and face. She was put into a Nursing Home after the incident. Finally, Ms. B's daughter came and took her out of the Nursing Home and now Ms. B is living in Florida with her daughter.

ANNA

Anna is a white woman, and she is 300 lbs. We all knew from the time Anna got there; she was not a good candidate. Anna has psychological problems; and she stated she had this problem at the age of 6 years old. She was staying in Long Island in a Hospital. I believe she ran away. Because she stated that some man wanted to take her away and that she was not going to be seen ever again. So, she ended up with us in the Shelter. Anna could not follow the rules, and she slept in the nude. Anna would go into the refrigerator and eat other people's food and that was not sitting well with the other ladies. She was told that she could not sleep in the nude, because there was another woman in the room with her. One morning, they saw Anna coming down the stairs to go to the bathroom with a sheet wrapped around her and no clothes on. She is on several medications. Her mother has an Order of Protection against her, and she is not allowed to go near her mother. She beat up her mother. While Anna was in the streets, Anna would sleep with total strangers just to get something to eat. Anna would sleep in the nude and come downstairs with a sheet wrapped around her. The Counselors told her that she could not sleep in the nude and that she had to respect the other roommates. The Counselors told her that they would try to get her a nightgown to sleep in. Anna stated that she would call her friend, Luke, and he would drive his car down the block and Anna would stay in the car while he went to her mother's house and ask to get her nightgown. Anna would sometimes put on the bright light in the room at 2:00 am to read the Bible and disturb the rest of her roommates and that was not sitting well with them. One cold Sunday morning, confusion started. Anna came downstairs

51

screaming and quoting scriptures from the Bible. She said that one of the Counselors was abusing her, because the Counselors wouldn't allow her to take her medication. She wanted a room for herself, which was unheard of, and she wanted the window open while the other roommates wanted the window close, because they were freezing. Anna started screaming. Anna and Shakira got into it that morning and the Counselors had to get in between the two of them or else it would have been a blood bath. The two of them were not backing down for anything. They tried to talk to her and calm her down and that was not happening. Anna started screaming, cursing and saying, "I am a beautiful Italian woman, and I make white beautiful babies and black people make fast food babies. (I cannot say the name of the fast-food restaurant, because of legal issues) We were black and uneducated, low class, and ghetto." She was out of control and one of the Counselors called the owner of the place and they told them to call the cops. On Sunday at 7:30 am, the cops showed up. They took her upstairs so she could pack her things. She said to the cops, "I want you to take me to the Station so I can make a phone call." The cops said, "No I'm not." Anna said, "Well, where am I going to go?" The cops said, "I don't know, and I don't care, "and the cops slammed the door in her face. The cops could see something was wrong with her. It was too early for all this drama. Christine peeped through the window, and they saw Anna walking down the streets with a garbage bag in her hand. Anna was never seen or heard from again. Christine felt bad for Anna. Anna said that to get something to eat, she had to sleep with strangers so she wouldn't go hungry.

SYLVIA

Sylvia is a middle-aged Spanish woman from Peru. She has a heavy accent and will not follow rules from anyone except her own rules. One of the rules in the Shelter is no one is allowed to use the stove except for the staff. Our meals are prepared by the staff for us every day. Sylvia came to Christine and asked if she had a lighter for her cigarette. Christine told her she did not smoke. Sylvia went and turned on the stove. The Counselors heard the clicking sound and Sylvia got yelled at. All she said was "I'm sorry." Sylvia again got in trouble. She was going on the bed to the top and she stepped on another person's clothes again and she said, "I'm sorry." There was a curfew at the Shelter. Sylvia, as usual, would not follow the rules again. Sylvia would often be late and as usual, she would say "I'm sorry." Sylvia crossed the streets, and she walked into the middle of the street and stopped the cars when they had the green light to cross the street. I guess she didn't know what the red traffic light was for. Well, we didn't see Sylvia for a few days. After crossing the street against the traffic light, Sylvia meets her faith. Sylvia was hit by a car twice. The only way her daughter would identify her body was from the tattoo on her arm. RIP (REST IN PARADISE SYLVIA).

MICHELLE

We had a new person that came in today and her name is Michelle. Michelle, a white woman 110 lbs., and 5'1" came into the Shelter. Michelle's father's neighbor dropped her off at the Shelter. Michelle had shingles when she came into the Shelter and did not tell anyone. Michelle is very educated, and Christine started talking with her and she said she was staying at another Facility. Again, I cannot mention the name of the Facility, because of legal reasons. Michelle said she has a son, and her mom lives in Florida. Her mom has custody of her son, and her dad lives in Long Island, so she told me. But Christine found out that her father was dead; and that she was living with her father's neighbor who lived upstairs. When the neighbor got tired of using her as his sex slave, he put her out. Michelle has anorexic problems and she's a heavy smoker and she smokes one pack of cigarettes a day and she drinks a lot of coffee. Michelle eats lots of canned vegetables, no sugar, no meat, no fish, and no vitamins. Michelle said her goal weight must be 90 pounds and it's making her crazy that she can't reach her weight. Michelle's menstrual cycle has stopped, because she's causing harm to her body. Michelle also stated that she sees a physiatrist for her problem. But Christine realizes that when she talks to her or anyone else, she knows she has a problem and she's very clever and she knows how to reverse her issues. Michelle is up all-night walking up and down, moving the bed, and making a lot of noise. The Counselors warned her about it, so the noise stopped. Michelle now sits at the dinner table and begs for money for her cigarettes, and coffee and borrows people's cell phones to make calls. She's a nice person, but she needs help. Michelle has shingles and never told anyone until she suffered a breakout. The Counselors called the ambulance, and they took her to the Hospital for the shingles and from there she was placed in a hotel. The Agency gave Michelle money to pay for her hotel stay, but Michelle took the money and ran. No one has seen or heard from Michelle again.

SHELIA

Christine met Shelia at the Shelter, and she asked her why she was here. Her story was that she was involved in a car accident. Because of the car accident, Shelia suffered seizures, and she was not allowed to go anywhere by herself. Shelia sued and got a settlement. Shelia got a new boyfriend, and this boyfriend, convinced her to take her money and invest it in a Store, so they could sell things. They were selling things including drugs. There was a raid in the Store and the boyfriend got arrested. He was sent to prison. Shelia was sent to prison to serve nine months. While in prison, Shelia saw women having sex with each other. Shelia came out and went straight into the Shelter. She finally got her life together and she has a new boyfriend who takes good care of her and she's doing great. Shelia arrived home one day, and she couldn't open the door no matter how hard she pushed the door, it would not open. Shelia finally decided to call the Police Department the Police came and they had to break the door down. Behind the door, Shelia's boyfriend was lying behind the door dead. The boyfriend's family did not want to bury him. Christine spoke to Shelia a couple of months before and Christine told her to get life insurance for her boyfriend. Shelia took her advice and that's what she used to bury her boyfriend. He was cremated and the boyfriend's children came and asked Shelia if he had life insurance and Shelia told them he didn't have any insurance. The rest of the insurance money she kept for herself. Shelia went to therapy and is doing great.

TERRY

There was Terry and she was adopted. Terry's mother tried to kill herself while she was pregnant with Terry. As soon as Terry was born, they took her away from her mother. Terry was adopted by a black family. There wasn't any love for her growing up, because she was a meal ticket for the family that adopted her. Terry was also sexually abused, and she had Abandonment Issues. However, Terry did get the chance to attend College. After College, she got a job at a Bank. Terry stole money from the Bank and ran away.

Terry got pregnant and her first child was a boy. The relationship didn't last so she's collecting child support, and her adoptive mother is taking care of her son while she runs the street. Terry is knee-deep in black magic (voodoo). Terry is now used to using men and women for money and worldly possessions. Once she gets what she wants, she sneaks out in the middle of the night and is never heard from again. She left men and women with broken hearts and no money. Terry met her next victim online and they hooked up. He was a Personal Trainer, Anthony, and he got her to go to school and she became a Licensed Personal Trainer. Soon they started training clients at the same gym together. Anthony would go out and get all the clients and he would share the clients with her. Everything was going smoothly so he thought. Eventually, Terry got pregnant by the trainer Anthony. Everything was going fine until she wanted money and more money. He started working double shifts just to satisfy her. She was not satisfied, and she was stressing him out. The people around him told him you're working too much and to relax. Since Terry was into black magic (voodoo), she knew his weakness. Behind closed doors, she would always put him down. She would beat him with a stick, slap him in the face, and would bully him if the money was not enough. There was a lot of fighting and arguing behind closed doors. Anthony had a plan, because he couldn't take it anymore. What Anthony didn't know is that Terry had a very checkered past, because she was a dancer, a bottle girl, a prostitute, and a scammer. He left and went to another country far away. Now they're communicating through texts, emails, and Facetime. Terry had a baby boy for Anthony to come back from overseas.

After two years, now Anthony hired a Private Detective to follow her, because he didn't trust her. Anthony found out that she was having sex with his boyfriend. Anthony is what you call (A down-low brother) someone who has sex with other men, but they're very discrete about it. Terry was also sending sexy pictures to Anthony's friends. She also had sex with Anthony's brother. Anthony is married to another woman in another Country, but he never told Terry he was married. They bought each other a ring and they said they were married. Terry is planning to take him to Court for Child Support and Alimony. Terry was evicted from her house; and the police are involved, because she's a bad parent and she's now homeless and on opioids and running the street selling her body and has STDs. Terry entered the Shelter, but she didn't last long, because she wanted to do what she wanted and not listen. Terry left the Shelter and ran the streets. Terry got pregnant again, but she suffered a miscarriage. Anthony has a feeling that the baby is not his and when Anthony wanted to leave, she starts crying. Christine ran into Anthony, and he looked like a stressed-out stray dog. Christine didn't know how much longer Anthony will put up with this relationship. A friend ran into Terry and she's currently living in her car. Terry is waiting for Anthony to buy her a house for her and Anthony's son. Anthony has plans to take his son away from Terry, because she's a bad mother. Anthony is planning to take her to Court before his son ends up in the System.

CAROLYN

Carolyn is one of the women in the Shelter. Carolyn took Christine under her wing and Christine got a vast amount of information like there is a Pantry and this Pantry is funded by the Government. In this Pantry, Christine visited, and the food is very good. It's better than the Shelter they were staying in. They treat everyone with love, kindness, compassion, and most of all with the utmost respect.

The Pantry is full of information. You can get your mail delivered there if you're homeless and they can help you get your Birth Certificate from anywhere in the world. One of the women who was in the Shelter with us is German and she got her Birth Certificate from there, but there is a fee of $50.00. They also provide people with hot showers, and toiletries for their use. As you transition back into the workforce, they will also provide you with a brand-new bedroom set and a living room set with all the proper documents.

From what Christine saw so far by coming to the Pantry regularly, there are people from all walks of life. There are Black, White, Spanish, Chinese, and Christine, who you never think would be there. There are the disabled, veterans, college students, working-class people, middle-class people, upper-class people, homeless people, drug addicts, and people with kids. Then you have the users and the abusers and don't forget the greedy and the pushy people. Christine decided that in her spare time, she was going to volunteer there for a couple of hours a day.

Some of the people who worked at the Pantry are volunteers and they were once homeless themselves and some lived in the Shelter where Christine lived. It's nice to see that they got on their feet and didn't walk away, but they decided to give back and help with their time which is very appreciative.

Christine realized that most of the people who are at the Shelter and in the Pantry, go out of their way to help you with any information they've gathered; especially if you don't have the information, they are still very kind to you.

As for Christine, she enrolled in a Nursing Course and graduated and is working and she has her very own apartment. Christine is out of the Shelter. It was a learning lesson and a learning experience for her. Christine finally decided to get herself together and she decided to join a gym, and she hired a Personal Trainer at the gym. Christine paid the gym membership monthly plus the Trainer fee which was monthly.

Christine noticed the Trainer would give her more training than any of the other clients. They started to get close, and they talked about each other families, food, drinks, and music. They followed each other on different social media platforms. When the Trainer gave Christine a heavy weight in frustration, Christine would say "Oh my God". The trainer would get angry and say why are you always saying, "Oh my God." She would ignore him.

Finally, the Trainer, whose name was Seth, asked Christine out and she told him "No", she had to work. She also told Seth that she would rather keep it professional, because she was not ready for a relationship. Seth did not know that Christine was very intuitive. Christine ended the training sessions with Seth, and she cancelled the gym membership. Seth, the trainer, unfollowed Christine from his social media account and Christine blocked and deleted his number from her phone. Christine thought that this was the end, but little did she know, trouble had just started.

Seth, the trainer, was a narcissist. He was very handsome and 49 years old and all the women were all over him at the gym. Christine realized that Seth wore a mask when he worked at the gym. He was a member of a Cult and Seth thought Christine would be a good fit to join the Satanic Sex Cult. The reason Seth asked Christine out was that he wanted to drug her and force her into sex trafficking and ship her to another Country. He was promised a lot of money if he delivered her. Again, Seth thought Christine was an easy target. Seth would call Christine from burner phones, and it would always be from different phone numbers and different Countries.

The Countries were:

Poland

Sir Lanka

Enosburg Falls, VT

Wellfleet, MA

Brewster, NY

Rhinebeck, NY

Las Vegas, NY

Salamanca, NY

River Hills WI

Angola, NY Bristol, TN

Laurel, MS

Nashville, TN

New Orleans, LA

Moorhead, MA

Phoenix, AZ

Benson, NC

Durham, NC

Canada

Seth belongs to an organization that was a Satanic Sex Cult where everyone who wanted to join, had to sell their souls and worship the devil. Seth sold his soul, and he wanted to be rich and popular. He also played football, and he was a semi-pro football player. Seth married a high-end prostitute/stripper.

Together they went on a rampage.
They would Steal from people

Rob people

Drug people

Kill people

Sell drugs for the Cartel

Dope people

Sex traffic (adults/children) Ponzi schemes

Steal vehicles

Break into homes

Taking out PP Loans in people's names including my
name

Steal identity

Seth was known as the Tinder Swindler. He would go on
dates with people on the dating website. Once they're together,
he would rob them of their money, checks, and credit cards when
they're in the bathroom washing up. Most of the people he met
were married, so they couldn't do anything.

Seth's wife, whose name is Pat, went as far as to get
cosmetic surgery to look like Christine, they had the same skin
complexion, but their height was different. She would go to
Mexico to get butt injections and breast implants.

They were both Cult Members and were all involved in
having sex with each other men with men, women with women,
or men and women. They were all passing different STDS
including AIDS. In this culture, organizations were made up
of professional football players, basketball players, attorneys,
doctors, police officers, and other people. Seth thought Christine
would be a good fit for their organization, but he was wrong.

Christine started putting Seth and his organization on
blast on social media. Seth got wind of it, and he paid someone
to destroy her platform. Christine created another platform (she
is a content creator) and now she's being shadow band. The only
Countries where Christine can get followers from are Africa and
Haiti. Seth is trying to get Christine off social media, but he
cannot, because Christine is following all the rules that come
with social media.

Seth's wife started going to the Police Station and filing false reports regarding Christine. The Police Officers did their research, and they realized that she was lying, and they told her that if she came back, they'd arrest her. Seth also married another person under a false name and he's a world traveler. The crime spree that they would go on, they would rob people and leave fake IDs with Christine's name and picture on them. They were also affiliated with different gangs and the color they wore was red.

Coming from the Homeless Shelter, Christine got herself a studio apartment and she leased a vehicle. Seth sent someone to put a nail in Christine's vehicle's tire, there was also a tracking device on her vehicle, they scratched and broke into her vehicle. Sometimes Christine would find herself taking the long way home after work instead of taking the parkway. Christine was led to take the long way home. They were waiting for her to cause an accident so they could rob her, shoot her in the head and they would then take pictures of her brains oozing from her head, or kidnap her. Once the lease was up on Christine's vehicle, Christine was very happy to return the vehicle back to the dealership.

Christine was followed everywhere she went. Christine went to get a manicure and pedicure, and women followed her into the salon. Christine went food shopping, and they followed her inside the grocery store, or they would wait for her outside or in the parking lot. Christine and her friends went to the beach, and they were six feet away from her just watching. Also, they would follow Christine to the gym.

The Cult Organization ordered a hit on Christine. One hitman came and he saw Christine and he fell in love with her, so he couldn't harm her. The other hitman got pulled over by cops, because he had warrants for his arrest and he was taken to jail, the other man took the money and ran away, and the other man got pulled over and had drugs in his vehicle and he was also taken to jail. Again, Christine life was saved.

The Cult Organization sent someone to steal Christine's mail from her mailbox. They re-routed her mail to a different address, so Christine went to the Post Office and got a post box. Christine is still not getting most of her mail, not even the junk mail. Pictures are taken of Christine and so are videos.

The Cult Organization was watching Christine everywhere she went, and the Feds were watching The Cult Organization watch her. The Cult Organization moved into Christine's neighborhood, and they were staying two doors down from her. At night, they would park in front of her home. They would come and kick the door, because they had planned to rob and rape Christine. Because of God, Christine was saved.

Seth and Pat were a very materialistic couple, and they only shopped at expensive stores and wore name-brand clothes. Because of their sexual habits, they engaged in gay for pay, they had sex in hotels, motels, and abandoned buildings, they had dates on several dating websites, and they also engaged in group sex, orgies, threesomes, tantrum sex, and anything else. They had favors from Judges, Attorneys, Detectives, and Police Officers.

Seth and Pat both have mental illnesses, STDs, and AIDS. They are going from riches to rags. It's only just a matter of time before whosoever is involved will go to jail and will die of AIDS.

Christine must go to Court and she must testify, because of what they did to her, by stalking her, which is illegal, by casting witchcraft spells on the Judicial System so that their Court dates would slow down, and some would be thrown out, also by using her name to take out loans for vehicles, homes, and PP loans, by writing false reports and by using her pictures to steal. The Feds moved into Christine's neighborhood and they're looking at the Cult Organization watching Christine.

Everyone has a story to tell. Never judge anyone you come across, because they're going through something. Don't be so quick to judge until you hear their story.

THE END

www.ingramcontent.com/pod-product-compliance
Lightning Source LLC
Chambersburg PA
CBHW020336130626
46549CB00003B/1196